SIMPLE SCIENCE SAYS:
Take One Magnifying Glass

SIMPLE SCIENCE SAYS:
Take One Magnifying Glass

by Melvin Berger

illustrated by
G. Brian Karas

SCHOLASTIC INC.

New York   Toronto   London   Auckland   Sydney

ISBN 0-590-42385-1

12 11 10 9 8 7 6 5 4 3 2   0 1 2 3/9
Printed in the U.S.A.   11

First Scholastic printing, October 1989

Contents

You can see lots of things with your eyes alone.

A ballpoint pen.

A leafy plant.

A painting.

A pair of shoes.

But you can't see *everything*.
Your eyes can't see—

the little ball at the tip of the pen,

the tiny veins in the leaves,

every brush stroke in the painting,

the many bits of dirt stuck to the shoes.

To see very small objects you need help.
You need something that makes things look larger.
Such a helper is called a *magnifying glass*.
Another name for a magnifying glass is *magnifier*.

Magnifiers make things seem larger
than they really are.
They give you a new way to look at the world!

SIMPLE SCIENCE SAYS:
Take the magnifier
from the back of the book...
and let's find out what it can do.

Slip the magnifier out of its case
almost all the way.
Hold the case like a handle
and look through the magnifier.
Touching the magnifier may make it dirty
and hard to use.
Keep the magnifier in its case
when you're not using it.

Notice how one side of the magnifier is smooth
and one side has ridges.
Hold the magnifier
with the *smooth* side facing down.
It works better that way.

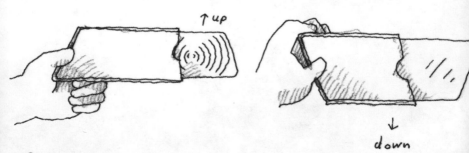

SIMPLE SCIENCE SAYS:
Surprise your eyes.

Turn to the picture on the cover of this book.
Look at it with your eyes alone.

Take another look.
Only this time use your magnifier
and look closely at one part of the picture.
Does the picture seem different?

It sure does!
Most of the lines that look straight
to the naked eye are actually uneven.
Some have bumpy, jagged edges.
The colors are not always inside the lines.
Often they spill over the sides of the drawing.

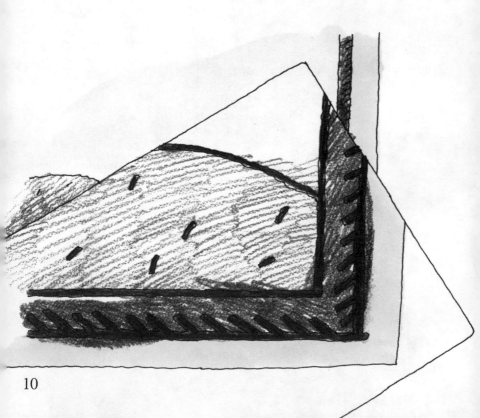

Now get a newspaper picture to look at.
Use your eyes.
Then take a closer look through the magnifier.

What do you find?
The picture is not solid at all.
It is made up of many teeny, tiny dots!

Pictures in newspapers are printed this way:
First workers cover the original picture
with a screen that has many small openings.
Then they photograph the picture
through the screen.
The screen breaks the solid colors into small dots.
These dots show up on the photograph.

Printers next make a metal plate from the photo.
The printing press spreads ink on the metal plate
and pushes it against the paper.
The final printed picture
is made up only of dots!

Where the color is dark the dots are large
and close together.
Sometimes they run into one another.
Where the color is light the dots are small
and farther apart.
Tiny dots that are far apart show hardly any color.

Now find a postage stamp of a single color.
Try to locate one that is fresh and new.
Use the magnifier to get "inside" the picture.

Surprise!
The color is not formed from dots.
It is made up of very fine lines.

The lines of the stamp design are cut
into a metal plate.
This is called engraving.
To print the stamp the lines are filled in
with ink and pressed on paper.

12

Now find a stamp that has many colors.
What do you notice through the magnifier?

The colors are built up of little dots—
just like the newspaper picture.
But it may be hard to see the dots on the stamp.
Sometimes it's easier to spot them
along the edges of the picture.

Here's another surprise in the stamp.
Move the magnifier around the border.
Do you see where the stamp was torn away
from other stamps?
Look for threads sticking out
along the ragged edges.
Stamps are printed on paper
made from wood fibers.
When the stamps are ripped apart,
the edges show the broken ends
of these wood fibers.

SIMPLE SCIENCE SAYS:
Examine your hands and fingers.

Study the back of your hand by eye.
It probably looks nice and smooth.
Now hold the magnifier
between your eyes and hand.
What do you see?

Your hand is crisscrossed with many tiny lines.
Maybe you can even see some very short hairs.

Flip your hand over and look at your palm.
When magnified, it shows some very deep lines.
The lines run in all directions.

Move into super-strong light.
Again look closely at your palm
through the magnifier.
Do you see lots of tiny holes?

These very small openings in the skin are pores.
The pores help your body to cool off.

Sweat (or perspiration) oozes out
through the body's pores when you're hot.
But the sweat soon dries up.
As it dries you feel a little cooler.

SIMPLE SCIENCE SAYS:
Take your fingerprints.

Like everybody else, you have a pattern
of tiny lines on each fingertip.
The pattern makes up your fingerprint.
It is important because it is yours alone.
No two fingerprints in the whole world
are exactly the same!

Taking your fingerprints is easy to do.
All you need is an ink pad,
some large index cards,
and a roll of paper towels.

Start with your right thumb.
Roll the tip back and forth on an ink pad.
Go from nail to nail.
Then slowly roll your inked thumb one time
on an index card.

Be careful not to smudge the print.
Once you have made a good print,
wipe the ink off your thumb with a paper towel.
Repeat the same steps with
each of your other fingers.

Use different cards to take fingerprints
of your family.
Label each card with the person's name.

19

Take a close look at the prints with your magnifier.
All fingerprints are of three basic types.

The loop: Lines start on one side,
loop around the center,
and end on the same side as they started.

The arch: Lines cross from side to side
with a rise in the middle.

The whorl: Lines circle around a central point.
Mark each print with an L (for loop),
A (for arch), or W (for whorl).

Which fingerprint type
is most common in your family?

SIMPLE SCIENCE SAYS:
Solve money mysteries.

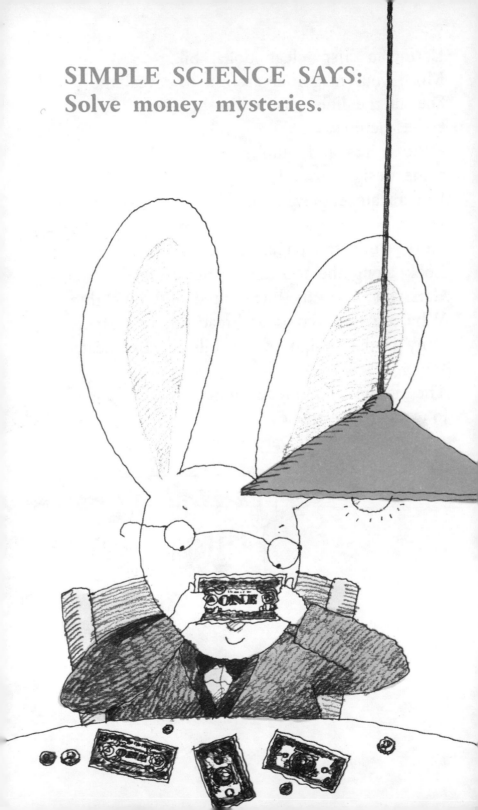

Borrow a crisp, clean dollar bill.
Move your magnifier around to reveal the details.
See all the lines that make up—
• the pictures,
• the words and numbers,
• the design around the edge.
Dollars are engraved, just like one-color stamps.

Next, study the paper itself.
Look along the top and bottom edges.
Can you spot tiny bits of red and blue thread?
Why are there colored threads in the paper?
Why is the design of the bill so complicated?

The design and threads make it very hard
to copy paper money.
And they make it very easy to spot a fake bill.

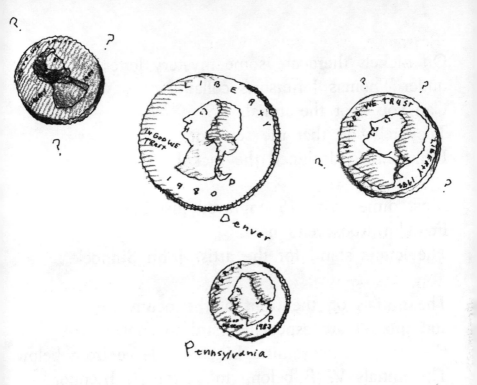

Denver

Pennsylvania

Coins, too, have mysteries that can be solved
with the magnifier.
Collect some bright, shiny pennies, nickels,
dimes, and quarters.
Use your magnifier to see what's hiding there.

Most coins—except pennies—
have a tiny raised *D* or *P*
in the lower part of the front side.
A *D* tells you the coin was made
at the U.S. mint in Denver, Colorado.
A *P* shows that the coin comes from the mint
in Philadelphia, Pennsylvania.
Do you have a coin without either of these letters?
That coin was probably minted in Philadelphia. 23

On nickels there are some mystery letters
under Thomas Jefferson's collar.
Can you spot the initials *FS*?
They tell you that the sculptor
Felix Schlag designed the nickel.

Most dimes have *JS* engraved just below
Franklin Roosevelt's neck.
The letters stand for the artist John Sinnock.

The initials on the front of the penny
and quarter are especially hard to spot.
For the penny, examine Lincoln's sleeve from below.
The initials *VDB* belong to Victor D. Brenner.

Peek up at George Washington's neck
on the quarter.
Cut into the tiny ridge are the initials *JF*.
John Flanagan created this coin.

SIMPLE SCIENCE SAYS:
Look closely at bugs.

Search your house or garage for a dead ant,
fly, mosquito, spider, or beetle.
Check around light bulbs and in dusty corners.

Put the bug on a piece of clean white paper.
And look at it through your magnifier.

Suppose you found a dead ant.
Like all insects it has six legs,
and its body is divided into three sections.
You should be able to see all three parts
with your magnifier.

Two feelers, or antennas, stick out from its head.
Since ants don't have noses,
they smell with their antennas.

Did you find a fly?
Note the huge eyes on both sides of its head.
The eyes can spot danger coming from
almost any direction.
Is it any wonder that most flies get away
before you can swat them?

Find the thin lines in the fly's wings.
They are veins.
Veins bring blood to the wings.
They also help to make the wing stiff enough
to push against the air.

What about a mosquito?
Can you see the long, skinny tube
sticking out of its head?
It's called the proboscis.
A mosquito bite is really a little stab
with its proboscis.

What does a close look at a spider or beetle reveal?

Collect two or three spoonfuls of soil
from out-of-doors.
Take the samples from different places.
Try to get some dark soil from a garden or lawn,
and some dirt that is very fine
from a beach or sandy lot.

Examine the garden soil through your magnifier.
Is anything mixed in with the soil?

Hairy bits of root?
Shreds of leaves?
Larger pebbles?
Anything creepy or crawly?

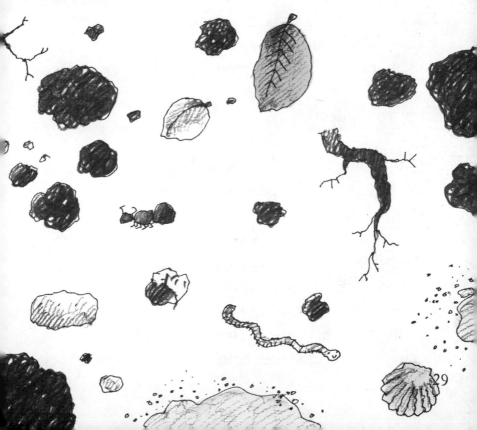

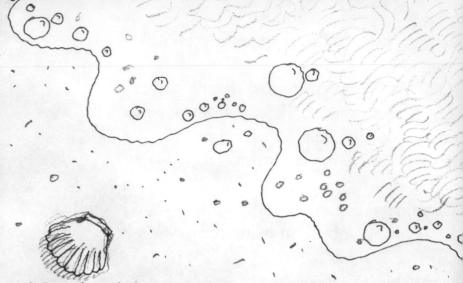

Most beaches or deserts are tan-colored.
But look at a little sand through your magnifier.
What do you find?

Close up, the grains are many colors—
white, black, brown, and red.
A few may even be green or yellow or gray.

Can you guess why?

Sand grains are really ground-up bits of rock.
The bits were chipped off big rocks
a long, long time ago.
Year after year after year
they rubbed against each other.
All this rubbing ground them down
into smaller and smaller bits.
Finally they became grains of sand.
Each grain keeps the color of the original rock.

SIMPLE SCIENCE SAYS:
See how birds keep dry.

Did you ever wonder why birds
never seem to get wet?
Their nests don't have roofs.
And many swim and dive all day
in lakes or ocean waters.

Find a feather and see for yourself
how birds keep dry.
Look at the feather through your magnifier.
Notice how the parts overlap like shingles on a roo
The overlap helps to keep the water off.

But feathers are waterproof in another way, too.
Drip some water on the feather.
Watch what happens.
The water runs off.
It doesn't make the feather wet.

The reason is simply this:
The feather is covered with oil.
And water slides right off oily things.

Crystals are chemicals with smooth, flat sides.
The sides meet in sharp edges.
Some crystals in your kitchen right now
are waiting to be discovered!

Table salt is one kind of crystal.
Sprinkle a few salt crystals on a dark,
flat, dry surface.
Look at them under your magnifier.
See how pretty and shiny they look!

Do the same with sugar and with instant coffee.
Each kind of crystal has its own shape.
And each one is very special.

Now look at pepper, flour,
and other powders found in the kitchen.
Do they look like crystals?
Most don't have the flat sides of crystals.

If there's snow where you live,
you can find some pretty crystals outdoors.
Dress warmly and go out with your magnifier.

Catch some snowflakes on your glove
or the sleeve of your coat.
Hold your breath and look at the snowflakes
through your magnifier.
(Your warm breath may fog the magnifier
and melt the snowflakes.)
Magnified snowflakes look quite amazing.
Each one has six sides or six branches.
And no two snowflakes are exactly the same!

35

Pour some table salt, a little at a time,
into half a glass of hot water.
Keep adding salt until no more will dissolve.
Dip a paint brush in the water
and paint a picture on a pane of glass.
A winter scene makes a very pretty picture.

Watch the pane through the magnifier.
After a while you'll see the water drying up.
It evaporates.
Soon only salt crystals are left
where you painted with the salt water.

Do you like the picture?
If not, wash the salt off the glass.
Try again.

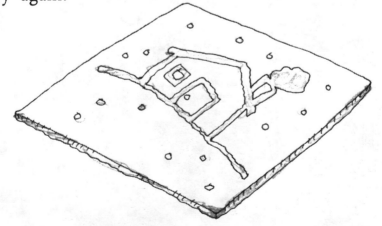

SIMPLE SCIENCE SAYS:
Watch food spoil.

Put a slice of bread on a dish.
Sprinkle water on the bread to make it moist.
Leave the dish in the air for a couple of hours.
Then cover it with plastic wrap
and set it in a warm, dark place.
Let it stay there for a few days.

After that time, take out the dish.
Pull off the plastic cover.
Is something fuzzy growing on the bread?

The fuzzy stuff is bread mold.
DON'T EAT IT!
Bread mold can make you very sick.

But the mold is very good for viewing.
Look at it under the magnifier.
The mold is a plant.
Like other plants, it has roots and branches.

Collect other kinds of mold if you can.
Mold usually grows on rotten or spoiled food.
How does each mold compare to bread mold?

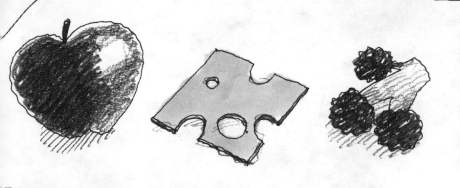

SIMPLE SCIENCE SAYS:
Make a magnifier picture.

Do this activity in the daytime.
Stand with your back to a window.
(It helps to keep the shades down
on the other windows.)

Hold the magnifier between the window
and a sheet of clean, white paper.
The scene through the window will show up
on the paper.
Move the magnifier back and forth
until the picture is clear.

But wait.
Something's wrong with the picture.
The tree has its leaves down and the trunk up.
The house is resting on its roof.
And the man is walking on his head.

Do you wonder why the magnifier
turned everything upside down?

Think of a tree outside your window.
The light from the leaves
passes through the magnifier—
and goes straight to the *bottom* of the paper.
The light from the trunks
passes through the magnifier—
and goes straight to the *top* of the paper.
The crisscrossing rays of light
make magnifier pictures topsy-turvy!

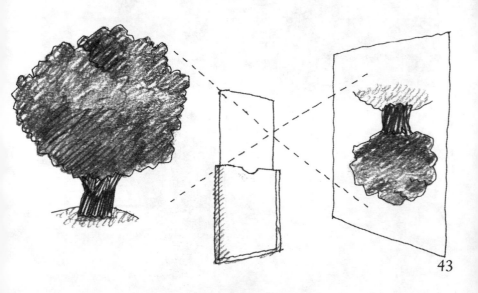

SIMPLE SCIENCE SAYS:
Put on a picture show.

ou can make a simple projector without much trouble.
ou'll need:

A large cardboard carton from the supermarket.

A big, bright flashlight.

A roll of tape.

Some photos or magazine pictures.

Your magnifier.

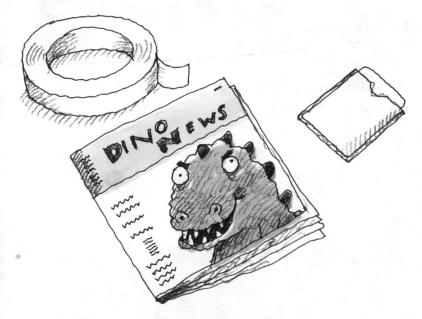

Set the carton on a table so that
the short end faces a blank wall.
Ask an adult to cut a small hole
in that side of the carton.
The hole should be at the bottom
and near the center.
Tape the magnifier across the inside of the hole.

Place the flashlight in the carton
but to one side of the hole.
The light should shine against
the inside back wall of the carton.
Hold a picture against the same wall.
Move the picture until you see a clear image
on the wall of the room.

Tape your
magnifier
to the inside
of the box
over the hole.

Put flashlight
in the box
facing away
from hole.

Now you're ready.
Slide other pictures into the same place,
one after the other.
Amaze your friends
with your magical picture show!

SIMPLE SCIENCE SAYS:
Take one magnifier—
and explore the exciting world
around you!